Running Home

John Caldwell

Copyright © 2015 John Caldwell

All rights reserved.

ISBN-10: 1518815871
ISBN-13: 978-1518815874

To all who have helped me become the man I am today, pointing me to Christ through life's painful circumstances…and to Shelby who never stops believing in me.

CONTENTS

	Acknowledgments	i
	Introduction	1
1	Beginnings	3
2	Passions	8
3	Your Future is a God Thing	15
4	The Pace of Grace	27
5	Sunday with Percy	32
6	Miracles on National	36
7	Looking Back	42
8	Real Life	45
9	Falling Apart	52
10	Running Home	69
11	Discovering Life	80
	About the Author	82
	Your Story	83

ACKNOWLEDGMENTS

Thank you to Fay, Larry, Ambur, Robb, Amy, Ki, and Ally Gossen, and Richard Romero, for loving me in a way that I have never been loved before. Thank you to Jeremy Henderson for showing me what God's love looks like. Finally, thank you to all who have influenced my life for the better. I am in awe of the way that you show God's love to the world around us.

INTRODUCTION

Have you ever got a speeding ticket? Luckily, I haven't yet, but I could only imagine what it would feel like. You just got your first car and you love it. It's the first time you take her out on the interstate and you're getting up to speed. You glance down at the speedometer and you realize that you're going about 15 miles per hour over the speed limit. At about the same moment, you realize that the guy who has been tailgating you for the last three miles is actually a cop, and the lights come on. You are terrified because you've never gotten a ticket before. You have no clue how much it will cost and you regret the lead that you secured to your right foot.

I hope this book is like your first speeding ticket. I bet you remember your first encounter with the law like the back of your hand. You just got your first enchilada of freedom and within the same month you got your first quesadilla of bills. No, I don't hope that you get a speeding ticket after reading this book. (However, that would be both ironic and hilarious.) No, I don't hope that you have unexpected bills pop up in the next couple of days. I would never wish any of that on you. My hope is that this book reminds you not to drive so fast in life that you miss out on living. I hope that this book inspires you to discover life at the pace of Grace.

1 BEGINNINGS

Life… Where do we even begin, you know? What is the meaning of our everyday lives? How do we live in a world so mundane, so ordinary? Is it really ordinary, or is it something extraordinary we have yet to discover? Can we find happiness in the midst of our sufferings? Can we allow ourselves to enjoy our lives under the weight of life's circumstances? These are the questions that I am hoping to answer throughout the course of this book.

My life began, like any other life, at a hospital. A place where physical grace is in action every day. People who are suffering come for healing. People who have physical disorders, mental disabilities, and even the common cold can come to a place where they are cared for and nurtured by nurses and doctors. It seems funny to me how our lives begin in a place that is surrounded by pain and suffering, however, we begin with wide eyes, open to things yet to be discovered. Our world is broken and in need of a doctor, a Healer. Our life begins in brokenness, yet as we grow old, by God's grace, we begin to live, and by life, love.

Growing up, my life was like any other young boy's life in Northern Arkansas. I lived in Hoxie, Arkansas, a town snuggled right next to a slightly bigger town named Walnut Ridge. It's funny thinking about it today; it was so long ago. The two towns absolutely hated each other even though the names of both towns were plastered on the same sign as you entered the area. Walnut Ridge was the better of the two with a population totaling around 4,500. Then there's Hoxie, the abandoned train epicenter of the area with a population of 2,000 or so. Don't get me wrong, we still had trains, but they never stopped there. They just blew their horns at midnight every weekday to wake up the entire town as they passed through.

Our house was a humble abode, a fixer upper if you will. There were lots of things wrong with it. The roof leaked, the floor was wavy because the foundation wasn't stable. The ceiling over my bed even had a hole in it covered by a thin piece of plywood. A piece of plywood so thin that you could hear the cats that would often reside in our attic. It was a good home though. To me, it represented my dad's desire to provide for his family and my mother's sanctuary in which she cultivated our lives. It was a growing ground for my sister and I.

When I was in second grade my sister was in tenth. We rode the same bus to school, and we would often have really awesome conversations, sometimes funny and sometimes serious. It was on those bus rides that we really began to grow our relationship. Sometimes I look back on those days. I remember those times with great joy in my heart. My seven-year-old heart had just begun to learn what it means to love.

As life moved on in those early years of my life, I began to discover what it means to love people despite the differences each of them represented. Today, I am still learning what it means to truly love someone, like Jesus does. At a young age, I realized that I was different from my peers. At school, I would try to talk to my classmates about Jesus. My little seven-year-old heart thought that everyone knew who Jesus was and everyone was hoping to go to heaven. I thought that everyone went to Church on Sunday and everyone had that little old lady give them candy before the service.

My little heart would soon be burdened by classmates who didn't know what I was talking about. Classmates who, eventually, would tell me to stop talking about what I learned in Sunday school because they didn't want to hear it. As I grew older I became more and more in tune to what the world thought about our Savior. Some of my peers had parents who were atheists. Some were other religions that my developing brain couldn't quite understand. My little life of seven years was being shaken by something that would stay with me for decades. A passion for loving people as Jesus does started in my elementary school cafeteria, and continues as I write this today.

My church was the coolest place ever. It was the first place that I made friends, met old people, and heard about my Creator. New Beginnings Family Worship Center was just down the road from where we lived. We went there a couple of Sundays and ended up calling that church our home for several years. It was there that I discovered friendship, compassion, the importance of giving, and many other biblical principles that I carry with me today. It was also the place that I gave my heart to my Savior at the age of 8. Our church was home, and that is how it should be. A church should be like a Welcome Center for the entire world. "Welcome to

Everlasting Love!", "Welcome to New Life in Christ!", "Welcome to a Safe Place". These phrases would be great to use in our bulletins, you know. A church is meant to be a place where the lost are welcomed, the hurting are healed, and the oppressed are ushered into new relationship with the Master. I will always remember my first church and the impact that the people there had on my young life.

As I grew slightly older, I began to notice little tugs at my heart. These little tugs would develop into full on passions, hopes, and dreams that I would pursue for the rest of my life. It was through these times of development that my heart and life would be radically changed.

2 PASSIONS

What does it mean to be passionate about something? Does it mean that we like doing it? You know, "Do the thing, do the thing!!" Does it mean that we spend most of our time thinking about how to do something better, or do we feel it in the deepest part of our souls? There are a lot of books out there that would tell you that passions are developed as we learn about the world. There are also books that would tell you that our passions are just things that we like a lot. My thought on the subject of passion is that it comes from our Creator. It comes from a heart that is fully focused on what God would have us do in this world. It comes from a place of complete surrender to Christ. That is where our passions grow and our lives begin to have meaning and purpose.

When I was ten, shortly after my parents got divorced, I started to play piano. At first, I would tinker around the little keyboard that my sister had bought for piano lessons. Of course, she didn't like that I wanted to play it too. It was mostly because I was horrible at it. The only song that I knew how to play was Chopsticks, which was the song that my grandma had taught me. As I began to play more often, I started to try other things. I would try pressing one key instead of another. I would play some black keys with the whites. Most of the time, it didn't sound good, but sometimes it would sound wonderful. My ear was beginning to hear what beautiful music sounded like.

As I grew just a bit older, I began to play special songs at church. One song that I remember specifically was entitled "Draw Me". It went something like this:

Draw me, draw me Lord

And I'll come running back to you

Oh, draw me, draw me Lord

And I'll come running back to you

You alone are all I need

You are my destiny

You alone are all I need

In you I am complete

It's amazing to me how such a simple song has stuck with me for all these years. As I practiced more and more, I began to develop a passion for playing the piano and I even began to sing. I didn't know how I was learning so fast. I could literally hear a song on the radio and have the entire thing down in thirty minutes. Today, I can do it in about fifteen.

As my passion for music grew, my passion for people grew as well. It started with the people at my church. Shortly after my parents got divorced, we started attending another church about thirty minutes from our house. It was amazing to see how our lives changed during that transition. After the divorce, my dad became a zombie. It was so sad to see him the way he was. Before, he was so full of life, and so happy. Looking back on it now, I should have seen the divorce coming. My mother and sister would fight all the time. They would fight over the smallest of things. Screaming, yelling, and slammed doors would be the end of most nights at home. My father was the only one holding the family together. He was clueless as to what to do about all the fighting. If he sided with mom, sis would get upset. If he sided with sis, mom would leave. The months leading up to the divorce were hard, and the months after were even harder. It was during the months after that we found comfort in our church home. It was Nettleton Pentecostal Church and, of course, our Savior, that kept both of us spiritually alive.

Looking back, I kind of enjoyed this time, even though it was hard. It was a time that my dad and I had to grow our relationship. I remember late Wednesday nights when we would come to a Waffle House restaurant and eat. We went so often that the people there knew exactly what we would order as soon as we came in the door. We met Teresa, who was an older woman who had been working there for several years at the time. She was extraordinarily sweet and kind. She became a mother figure to me. I think she was one of the people that helped my dad mend his broken heart after the separation.

Ironically, years later, I am sitting in a Waffle House, sipping coffee, writing this book. It has become a place of restoration and meditation for me. I know, it's kind of odd, but I don't mind it. Come to think of it, a lot of wonderful things in my life have happened at a Waffle House. Waffle House is where I first wrote out my testimony (and cried). It is also the place that I started a blog with one of my good friends from high school. And, Waffle House is also the place that I first talked to Mike about Jesus.

Mike is a simple man, an older guy that really enjoys talking about deep things. Fast forward to just about a year ago. I first met Mike after our normal Wednesday evening service at One Life Church. As our Janitor, Mike knows a lot of us, especially the ones who are on the leadership side of things. He works long hours to ensure that all of the individual rooms, hallways, and corridors are properly clean and sanitary. He does such a wonderful job and we are so glad to have him. I was just coming out of the youth room after cleaning up our music and things from the service, when I noticed him. I saw him crossing the foyer and decided to introduce myself. You see, I am a people person through and through. If I don't know someone I will go out of my way to meet them. That is what I did with Mike.

We started talking, and we instantly hit it off. He shared with me things that were going on in his life, the good, the bad, and sometimes, even the not so pretty. We started to grow a relationship. I would say hi to him when I saw him during the week. No, I didn't stalk him. I actually had an internship with the Youth Pastor who is now my adopted brother. That's another story I will tell you later.

Mike and I were starting to become the best of friends. We would talk for hours about random life things. There were things that he needed to get off his chest, things that were worth celebrating, and things that were tough. He just needed a friend, and even though I was about a third of his age, I wanted to be that friend. Now, we often meet, after talking for hours at the church, at a Waffle House. We have coffee and talk about life. It was in these conversations that I introduced Mike to Jesus.

Passions grow in our hearts. Our passions are like seeds planted in the deepest depths of our souls. If they are watered, fed, and nurtured, they can grow into something as beautiful as the flowers in spring. They can flourish into something so beautiful that everyone that we come into contact with wants to harvest it for themselves. Our passions drive who we are and what we do with our lives. If our passion is to love people as Jesus does, those same people that we touch everyday will harvest the love Jesus has lavished on us and spread that same love to the world around us.

3 YOUR FUTURE IS A GOD THING

We discover life in the midst of brokenness, when it hurts and when it's hard to carry on. In this chapter I'm going to do something a little different, something that I don't think anyone has done before. I am working toward my Local Minister's License with the Church of the Nazarene and this Thursday, I will be sharing my first sermon with our College group! So, this chapter will be made up entirely of my first message. It is a message, I believe, will inspire you and encourage you to discover life at the pace of Grace.

"Your Future is a God Thing"

John's First Sermon

Jeremiah 29:1-14:

"Jeremiah wrote a letter from Jerusalem to the elders, priests, and all the people who had been exiled to Babylon by King Nebuchadnezzar. This was after King Jehoiachin, the queen mother, the court officials, the other officials of Judah, and all the craftsmen and artisans had been deported from Jerusalem. He sent the letter with Elasah son of Shaphan and Gemariah son of Hilkiah when they went to Babylon as King Zedekiah's ambassadors to Nebuchadnezzar. This is what Jeremiah's letter said:

'This is what the Lord of Heaven's Armies, the God of Israel, says to all the captives he has exiled to Babylon from Jerusalem: "Build homes and plan to stay. Plant gardens and eat the food they produce. Marry and have children. Then find spouses for them so that you may have many grandchildren. Multiply! Do not dwindle away. And work for the peace and prosperity of the city where I sent you into exile. Pray to the Lord for it, for its welfare will determine your welfare."

'This is what the Lord of Heaven's Armies, the God of Israel, says: "Do not let your prophets and fortune-tellers who are with you in the land of Babylon trick you. Do not listen to their dreams, because they are telling you lies in my name. I have not sent them," says the Lord.

'This is what the Lord says: "You will be in Babylon for seventy years. But then I will come and do for you all the good things I have promised, and will bring you home again. For I know the plans I have for you, "says the Lord. "They are plans for good and not for disaster, to give you a future and a hope. In those days when you pray, I will listen. If you look for me wholeheartedly, you will find me. I will be found by you," says the Lord. "I will end your captivity and restore your fortunes. I will gather you out of the nations where I sent you and will bring you home again to your own land." (NLT)

...I pray that through this message you are able to see God's grace flowing from the pages that follow. This was where I led the congregation in prayer before the message began...

Have you ever made plans with someone and it didn't go as well as you wanted it to? Well, I have. There was this one time that I made plans with a girl that I (not so) secretly had a crush on. I asked her out for coffee and she said yes. I was thrilled. I spent the days in between, dreaming about what our relationship could become, after this fateful first date. Then, the day came and I got extremely nervous so I did everything that a guy "should do" for a first date. I reserved us a table at the local Starbucks, I bought flowers for her, and I even put on my best clothes and my favorite cologne. As I pulled into the driveway that afternoon, my heart started pounding in my chest. Luckily she wasn't there yet so I had a few minutes to gather my thoughts. I walked towards the door and sat down. Then, she walked in sporting a T-Shirt and jeans while I was all dressed up. My face turned red as I looked over at the bouquet of flowers graciously sitting on the table. It was obvious that she did not think this was a date. I was beginning to realize that this wasn't going to turn out the way I had hoped.

Have you ever been there? You know, when something goes horribly wrong and you don't know what to do. You didn't plan for her to think this wasn't a date. I mean, it was supposed to go according to my plan, right? We'd go on a couple of dates, we'd get really close, and then the time would come where I would pop the question. That's exactly how I wanted it to happen. When things happen in life that we don't completely understand, when things don't go our way, it's hard to see through the chaos what God's plans are. We don't plan for our family to fall apart, we don't plan for our hearts to be broken, and we don't plan for our addiction to get out of control.

This is what the people who were exiled to Babylon were feeling. King Nebuchadnezzar had just ripped them away from everything that was familiar to them. They had no resources, no food, and no idea what to do. They were in exile. It was like going to a foreign country by yourself, without money, without a translator, and without hope of ever returning. It's in these times of our own exiles that we need to focus on what God told these people who were so desperate for a savior. We must remember that in our own personal exile: God's plans are good, God's plans protect us, and God's plans give us a future and hope.

1st Point: God's plans are good.

Jeremiah 29:4-7:

"This is what the Lord of Heaven's Armies, the God of Israel, says to all the captives he has exiled to Babylon to Jerusalem: 'Build homes, and plan to stay. Plant gardens, and eat the food they produce. Marry and have children. Then find spouses for them so that you may have many grandchildren. Multiply! Do no dwindle away! And work for the peace and prosperity of the city where I sent you into exile. Pray to the Lord for it, for its welfare will determine your welfare.'" (NLT)

Our text reveals to us that God's plans are good!! God didn't want the exiles to look back at what their lives had been before. He wanted them to build their lives right where they were. God directed the exiles to build families, grow food, marry, and have children. God created all of these beautiful things, and He wants us to experience them. God's plans for them were everything that we value in our own lives today, but in the midst of their griping and complaining, they didn't realize the blessings that were right there in front of them. I value all of the wonderful people God has brought into my life and one day, I will value my wife, kids, grandkids, and even hopefully great grandkids. God's plans for us are all good and only good, but it is so easy to get distracted from what God has in store for our lives. In your own personal exile remember that God's plans are always to grow and mature your faith, despite your circumstances. We experience hurt and pain, but God's going to turn it around for good. We encounter places in our lives where we have no idea where God is. We battle depression, deal with family issues, or try to fight an addiction on our own. We have to remember that God is right there in the midst of our pain. He knows what we are going through, He loves us with an everlasting love, he holds us up out of the stormy waters, and He has plans for us that we could never even dream of. His plans for us are far beyond the chains of addiction, depression, or anything that we may be facing. His plans surpass every plan that we have ever made. And, most importantly, His plans don't go horribly wrong like mine did with my first date. Not only are God's plans all good and only good, but God's plans protect us from things we don't even know are bad for us.

2. God's plans protect us

Jeremiah 29:8-10:

"This is what the Lord of Heaven's Armies, the God of Israel, says: 'Do not let your prophets and fortune tellers who are with you in the land of Babylon trick you. Do not listen to their dreams, because they are telling you lies in my name. I have not sent them,' says the Lord."

"This is what the Lord says: 'You will be in Babylon for seventy years. But then I will come and do for you all the good things I have promised, and I will bring you home again."(NLT)

The exiles in Babylon thought that God had raised up these fortune-tellers. They were fooled and they didn't even know it. These fortune-tellers were giving the people false hope in the midst of exile. Doesn't that sound familiar? In our own lives we have moments where we think that certain things, or situations will satisfy our hunger for hope. We think that we can go to that website to relieve our pain, we think that we can solve family situations on our own, and we think that we can succeed from our own effort. The good news is: Our Savior doesn't abandon us when we fall into sin.

Jesus is the one who doesn't abandon us when we cave in to that addiction. He doesn't abandon us when we aren't the person that He called us to be. Jesus has a heart that longs for us to be in close relationship with Him every single day. He longs for us to be strong enough in Him that we don't fall for the tricks of the enemy. That's what his plans are, his plans are for us to be so close to Him that everything else, all of our worries, our finances, and even our addictions yield in response to The Master. As we grow in this relationship with Christ, He continues to pour into us so that we can spread His hope to other people. He gives us hope in the midst of our troubles. He cares for us like a mother cares for a newborn. He provides for all of our needs, and he is sure to bring us away from the darkness of lies and trickery and in to the light of His love.

3rd Point: God's plans give us a future and hope

Jeremiah 29:11-14:

"For I know the plans I have for you", says the Lord. "They are plans for good and not for disaster, to give you a future and a hope. In those days when you pray, I will listen. If you look for me wholeheartedly, you will find me. I will be found by you," says the

Lord. "I will end your captivity and restore your fortunes. I will gather you out of nations where I sent you and will bring you home again to your own land." (NLT)

Our God will be found by us. What an intriguing statement. God didn't say, "I will reveal myself to you when you want me to, how you want me to, and where you want me to." No, He said, "I will be found by you." Finding something, or someone, requires the action of looking, seeking, and even crying out. Have you ever cried out for the remote? You know, that weird thing you do when you're trying to find it. "Heeeerrrre remote! Here boy! Heeeeeeere remote! I have new channels for you!!!"

You know, I have a feeling that the exiles weren't looking too hard for God. They were finding every reason to blame God for their circumstances. They were looking back to the good times they had back in Jerusalem before the exile. They were thinking back to when life was easy and predictable, but God wanted their trust, their entire devotion, their surrender. So how do we find God in the midst of our own personal chaos?

Psalm 46:10 gives us clear instructions on what to do in times of uncertainty…

"Be still and know that I am God. I will be honored by every nation, I will be honored throughout the world."

Our plans should be God's plan. God's plan for us is to bring Jesus to the least and the lost, the ones who are embraced by society and the one who have been forgotten. We are to be the hands that reach out to the world around us. We are to be the feet that go to every nation to lift the name of Jesus high on every mountain top. We carry the responsibility to represent God's grace to the world around us.

I had no idea that I would be here, writing this book, a couple months ago when I was battling depression. I had no idea that I would be adopted by a wonderful family after I left home at 15. I was clueless in the midst of chaos. But, God wasn't. He knew exactly what he was doing. He was holding me in the palm of His hand, directing my path and ushering me in to right relationship with Him. I can't begin to count the number of divine appointments, what some people would call coincidences, that I have seen in my life. Praying with people in public places, receiving money from God-directed people to provide for bills I had to pay, and even finding money lying by my scooter when I didn't know where my next meal was coming from. These are what I call God things, and your future is a God thing. I'm not saying that you shouldn't make plans, but when you do make plans, put God first and foremost, and don't let your personal chaos get in the way.

Some of you are at a point in your life where you don't know what to do. You're at a crossroads where all the choices are bleak, scary, or impossible. You have no direction and no plan. I want to encourage you that God is right where you are. God is with you when you face this addiction, He is with you when you try to mend that family relationship, and He is with you through the darkness. He knows what you're facing and He's going to carry you through this. Don't worry about how it's going to happen, or when. It's all in His timing and His plan. Your future is a God thing.

My hope is that your heart was encouraged by my first message. I also hope that you were able to relate it to the topic of discovering life at the pace of Grace. God does have a plan, even when you don't understand. Your future is being crafted by the hands of the Master.

4 THE PACE OF GRACE

So, I did not plan to write this chapter at all. I actually planned to title this chapter "Falling Apart" and it would have talked about how my life started to crumble shortly after my parents got divorced. However, God had bigger plans for this chapter, so I guess that will have to be the title of another chapter.

As, I mentioned earlier, at this particular time in the course of writing this book, I was sitting at a Waffle House, typing away all of the beautiful words that had been flowing from the Master's heart to mine. I was about to head out the door when an older, paralyzed man scooted awkwardly in the door asking for a cup of water. I was intrigued by the man and so I glanced over before I got up from my table. I kept looking over as one of the waitresses went over to talk to him. She got him the cup of water that he requested, made him a meal, and asked what had brought him there this early in the morning. (As I am writing this, it is 2:29 am.) The woman ended up praying with him and asking if he had a place to go. He went on to explain how he had been released from the emergency room down the road after he got hit by a pizza delivery driver in the next town over. He was brought into the ER in Springfield and had no way to get back to his home in Republic.

Then, it dawned on me. I actually live off of the road that goes that direction. As I continued to listen to his story, he went on to explain how he wasn't able to call anyone at the hospital because of their "security procedures". Apparently the lady was very rude to him because of the color of his skin. I didn't know that this still happened in the United States. I was absolutely dumbfounded. Anyway, Waffle House graciously provided a phone, but he wasn't able to get into contact with the friends that he was staying with. I have never seen any man this age cry before, but it was heartbreaking. So, I inquired about where he was staying and offered to give him a ride home.

A million different things rushed through my mind in the next couple of minutes.

"What if he's faking it?"

"What if he's actually going to kill me and steal my car?"

"What am I going to do if he tries to hurt me?"

"What if, what if, what if???"

Then, a calming peace came over me as I helped him into the passenger side of my car. As I was closing the door, I looked up at God and smiled, knowing that this was definitely one of those "God Things". As I began to drive, Percy finished his dinner. I have never seen anyone eat eggs, bacon, and toast so fast in my life. He was so hungry and thirsty that he was inhaling what he had. I typed his address into my GPS and off we went.

As we drove into the night (now 1am), I began to talk to Percy. I asked him about his life and what he liked to do. He said that he once wanted to be a Pastor, but was looked upon as insufficient because of his paralysis from the waist down. My heart ached at that. I asked him if he had a bible and he quickly said no. He said that he had it all in his head. Wow, to be like him, to have memorized most of the bible not because I wanted to for fun, but because of necessity. I told him that we had to fix that "not having a bible" thing. We talked more about where he is staying and what the situation is like there. I asked him if he was comfortable going home because the way he explained his situation concerned me. He said that he was, so we continued in the direction of the address he gave me.

As we started to get closer, he told me to keep a look out for his wheelchair. That was the only way that he could get around. We went by the intersection where he had been hit, and we didn't see it. We did see the water bottle he had held in his hand before the accident, but no wheelchair. As we arrived at the house, I noticed something shiny reflecting the light from my headlights. It was his wheelchair sitting right next to the steps going up to the house. It was at this moment that my heart dropped. I have never seen someone so happy to see a wheelchair. This was his enchilada of freedom, his livelihood. Unfortunately, the chair had been mangled to a point where it seemed unrepairable. He was absolutely crushed. I assured him that I would work with the church to provide for him a new one. As I helped him up to the house as much as I could, one of his housemates came out to see what was going on. I introduced myself as one of the interns to college students at my church. She was excited to hear that I was from One Life because she had been there a couple of times a few years ago. I spent quite a few minutes talking with her and found out that she was in school and was in need of school supplies so I scavenged my car for what little I had in there. I had two paper real-estate folders, a notebook, a bag of chips from Panera that I never ate, and a pen. I ended up giving it all to her along with my bible to Percy. I prayed with the family and invited all of them to church on Sunday. When I offered to drive them, they excitedly accepted. They went on to explain how they hadn't been to church in a while, but so desperately wanted to come back. In the car ride over, Percy had told me that the people that he lives with do drugs, drink, and even have intimate relations with several different people.

As I am sitting here processing the events of tonight, my heart breaks for the family. I am in awe of what God has allowed me to do tonight. It is now 3 am and I have to work tomorrow, but I couldn't go to sleep without writing all of this down.

God is so good, isn't He? I talked about being the hands and feet of Christ in the previous chapter and this is a wonderful example of doing just that in our everyday lives. I hope you are as in awe of God as I am right now!!

5 SUNDAY WITH PERCY

The rest of the weekend passed by fairly quickly after I gave Percy a ride home Friday night. Saturday morning was definitely a bear because I had to be at work at nine thirty in the morning. It was definitely hard, but I know that God gave me the strength to get through the day.

Sunday morning came rather swiftly, almost too swift. I ended up accidently sleeping in on Sunday so I was a little late to pick Percy up for church. Luckily, I thought that the service started at 10:15 when in reality it started at 10:45. That was my saving grace.

As I struggled out of bed after a long night at work the day before, my heart was full of joy. I was so excited to be able to give people rides to church. This was actually the first time that I had gone to a stranger's house to pick someone up for church. I would have done this kind of thing a lot sooner if I had more than a 49cc scooter to get myself around. Anyway, as I crawled out of bed my phone went "ding". It was Barbara, Percy's friend from the other night. As I read the text, I was crushed. Barbara said that they weren't going to be able to come to church with me this morning. Curiously, I asked if Percy still wanted to come. Apparently, she was trying to keep him from coming.

Finally, I talked her into letting Percy come because he wanted to get one of the wheelchairs that had been donated to the church to replace his old one. I jumped in my car around 10:15 or so and headed toward Percy's house.

As I pulled into the driveway, I got slightly nervous again. These were complete strangers that I had not met until just days earlier. My stomach started to clinch as I knocked on the door.

"What if they don't want me here?"

"What if they answer the door with a gun?"

"What if they offer me drugs, or are high themselves?"

All of these thoughts flashed through my head. These thoughts were pre-conceived judgements that I had about these people, but God tells us in his word that what we do for the, "least of these" we have done for him. This is what we are called to do. We are called to bring in the "least of these", clothe them if they need clothes, feed them if they're hungry, and provide a bed if they have nowhere to stay.

Sometimes, as Christians, it is so easy to stay within our own little bubble. I admit, it is pretty comfortable in here. We love our church, we love the people, and we love the fellowship. It's like the best social club ever. However, we have to be careful not to put a membership policy on our church signs:

"You must have white skin, be in the middle to upper class, and have a loving family to join this church."

God calls us to be the hands that reach out to the outcasts of society. He calls us to usher them in to the place where forgiveness and grace are offered. He calls us to love them unconditionally, without our pre-conceived judgements.

Percy and I had a wonderful day Sunday. After church, he wheeled himself out into the foyer and out the door. On his way, he was greeted by some and looked down upon by others. It broke my heart to see people in my own congregation looking at him as if he had nothing to offer. Percy is the most passionate person I have ever met and he is paralyzed. I absolutely loved our time together and was so happy to have him in service with us. We had lunch at a Chinese restaurant close to the church. At first he wanted to go to McDonald's, but I told him about the Chinese restaurant that I love and he got excited about having shrimp fried rice for the first time in years. Percy is my friend and I am so glad to have met him. He has radically changed my viewpoint on reaching the lost and I hope that there are many more Percy's to come. Next Sunday, I will be going to pick him up for the service, and hopefully, his friends will come along too.

6 MIRACLES ON NATIONAL

Wow... I had no clue... Two months ago I bought my first car and now I am using it to minister to people. It was another one of those God things. Weeks before I bought it, I had been shopping around on Craigslist to no avail. All of the cars were either really cheap and sketchy, or they were out of my price range entirely. I was beginning to get discouraged. Then it dawned on me. I could apply for a loan!! It might be a long shot, but the worst they could say is no, right?

The search began the day after the light bulb came on. I started with the bank that currently supplied my checking account and credit card. I had high hopes, as I had been with the bank for about three years now. I thought that I had established quite the trust from them. When I went in to apply for a loan, the branch manager was so kind and courteous. She really knew how to give great customer service, and by the time I left, I really believed that I might have a chance.

The next day I was supposed to get a phone call from the branch manager telling me whether or not I got approved. I didn't get the call, so I went in and talked to her in person. I hung my head as she, politely as she could, told me that I was not approved. I was crushed. As I was pulling out of the parking lot, however, I remembered something that my dad had done growing up. When he got a loan for our house, he had shopped around for a bank. He wanted to get the best deal, and the best interest rate. So, I set out on a journey to find a bank that would give me a loan for my first car.

Finally, I landed at Old Missouri Bank. After getting denied at another bank, the loan officer there referred me to this one. She gave me the name and phone number of one of the loan officers that she knew personally. It sounded great and I was so excited! I called the guy the same day and ended up setting an appointment with him scheduled for the following Monday. The time in-between was spent in countless hours of prayer, asking God if this was Him. It was early fall and the cold winter months were approaching. My scooter was not winter proof, and was definitely on its last leg.

Monday morning, I walked through the doors of the bank, dressed up and ready to give my "I desperately need a car" speech. I checked in with the receptionist, and sat down after getting a free cup of coffee from the little kiosk by the door. I had practiced what I would say on the way over, and was starting to get a little nervous.

"I own a scooter that is not winter proof."

"I think that it might be on its last leg."

"Please help me...*falls to knees*"

These were just a few phrases that I wanted to incorporate in my loan pitch. Finally, as I finished my cup of coffee, the receptionist came out from the back and told me that, let's call him Jim, the loan officer I was supposed to meet with, had tried to get a hold of me in order to reschedule because something came up.

"Okay, that's kind of odd, because I don't remember getting his message", I thought.

I went on to ask the receptionist if there was someone else that I might be able to meet with. Monday was my only day off that week, and I wanted to get the ball rolling as soon as possible. The receptionist said that there were other loan officers available that would be able to help me, so after waiting for just a couple of minutes, I was in.

Sally, the loan officer that I ended up speaking with, was the most chipper loan officer I have ever met, especially after all of the banks that I had been to at this point. She was so happy that I had thought to come to their bank to get a loan for my first car. She ended up giving me an application and I was approved for the loan the same day. As we were finishing up the paper work, she asked if I had found a car yet. At this point, I hadn't actually found a car, but I knew the price range that I wanted to stay in. I told her that I hadn't and she perked up a little. She went on to tell me that she was looking to sell her personal car that she had had for seven plus years. That was the first sign that this was definitely a God thing. I asked her what kind of car it was and as soon as she said, "It's a 2003 Honda Accord, 2-door coupe, V6", *my* ears perked up. It almost sounded too good to be true. I asked her how much she wanted for it and she said that she would call her husband at lunch to talk to him about it. Then, we agreed that she would call me after she talked to him about the car.

At this point, I was already starting to downplay the whole thing. I thought that she would want too much for it, or something would go wrong with the loan. I was expecting my first car to be a total clunker. This car was definitely not a clunker. Before I left, she took me on a test drive. She offered to let me drive, but I declined because it had been so long since I had driven a car. I was afraid that I would wreck it before I even got it out of the parking lot. Thankfully, she understood and drove herself. As I opened the car door, my eyes got really big. It was the nicest car that I had ever seen that was this old. I didn't get too excited as I still didn't know what she wanted for it.

After the test drive, we came back to the bank and went inside. This is when she told me that she would sell the car for exactly what the bank would loan me for it. I was totally blown away!! At this point I knew, beyond the shadow of a doubt, that this was definitely a God thing. I called my adopted dad (another story I will share later), and told him everything that happened. He was so excited for me and told me that he would give me a ride to the closing the following Wednesday.

This was the first of many miracles that would happen on National Avenue in Springfield, Missouri. Just a couple of blocks down from the bank sits the little Waffle House where I met Percy and Shawn, two men that needed a ride home on separate occasions. Waffle House is also where I met Deborah, a waitress there, who brings me free coffee every single time I come in to write. She is such a sweet lady. When I told her that I was writing a book, she got so excited that she wanted me to write down all the information for her. It was at a Waffle House restaurant that I spent a lot of my time with my dad, and it warms my heart to return to one and write my story.

7 LOOKING BACK

This might turn into the hardest chapter to write thus far along our journey. If you remember, I dropped a couple of hints that I would be talking about my life growing up. Life after my parents got divorced was very hard. It was a time filled with uncertainty and pain. My father turned into a zombie after the divorce. He didn't know what to do. His heart was so broken that it seemed as if he had lost his ability to love. During this time, we tried to grow our relationship, but I could tell that he was trying to be strong for me. He didn't show that he was completely broken on the inside. He tried so hard to act like everything was okay, to be my rock. Deep down, I could tell that the divorce had taken its toll on his heart and his life.

Waffle House became a place that both of us loved. It wasn't really for the food, or the coffee (although very delicious). No, it was for the company that we found there. Teresa, the older waitress that we met there became like a mom to both of us. She would always ask how we are doing and truly showed that she cared for us.

The days after the divorce were also very complicated. My dad was putting himself through school in his early 40s, and it was not a very good financial situation for the two of us. Some nights all that we would have to eat would be canned Pork 'N Beans. Among other cheap things, Ramen Noodles consisted of a lot of our meals. It broke my heart to see my dad this way. He was trying so hard to keep it together. He tried not to show his pain, but there would be nights, after I was supposed to be in bed, that I would listen, next to his bedroom door, as he cried himself to sleep. I would ask myself:

"Why did this have to happen?"

"Why did mom have to leave?"

"What can I do to make my daddy feel better?"

These questions haunted me as I went throughout my daily life. My grades fell tremendously in this time, mostly because I would catch myself thinking about what I could do when I got home that might make my dad feel better.

"Should I make a card, just telling him that I love him and I'm proud of him?"

"Should I just run up to him and give him a big ole bear hug?"

My little heart just wanted to see my dad smile again. I just wanted to know that he was okay and that we could get through this together. He was so lonely, and I just wanted to be there for him.

My heart aches as I am writing this. Today, we don't talk that much, but someday, I hope that our relationship will be renewed. I have prayed so much for my father and the new family that he has started with my step-mother. I pray that one day, we will have a good relationship again, but until that happens, I will keep praying and keep trusting God to give me peace in the midst of chaos.

8 REAL LIFE

Real life isn't always pretty. Real life encounters difficult situations, hard times, and heartbreaking news. This chapter is the written version of my testimony that I talked about earlier. I wrote this, ironically, sitting in a Waffle House, just about a year ago. I hope that you receive hope through my story and that you can see that God has big plans for your life as well as mine.

Every time I see the sunrise, it reminds me of the power and might of our Lord, Jesus Christ. I often have this shrinking feeling, like the world around me is just a small glimpse of how great our God is. God has brought me through what feels like the impossible. Through all of these trials, I know He has big plans for my life. Let me take you through the journey of my testimony. I think you will get quite a blessing from it.

I had an interesting childhood. At first, my parents were happily married with my sister (eight years older) and me. We lived in a very humble abode. The floors were uneven in most places. My room even had a piece of plywood covering a gaping hole in the ceiling. It was rough. My mother and sister would fight constantly, leaving my dad in the middle to be the mediator, while I watched on the sidelines, taking note of what not to do. The house that we lived in didn't have central heat and air. Needless to say, the fall and spring months were warmly welcomed. Life at this point was alright.

My tenth birthday came and things started to change. I will never forget my birthday get together at the local Pizza Hut. I was so excited to have a Birthday cake with a classic car on it, but I noticed something. My mom wasn't there. My father and sister were, but they mentioned nothing about it.

My mom ended up in the mental hospital. At the age of ten, I really didn't understand. I remember going to the hospital and not being able to see my mom, for some reason. She would send gifts with my dad, but I didn't understand why she couldn't give them to me herself. Then, my mom went on "vacation". The conversation went something like this.

"Why isn't mommy here?"

"She's going away for a while. She'll be back just to see you, OK?"

"But, I want to go with her!!!! I don't understand!"

"She'll be back, okay? Don't worry."

She didn't come back, well, not permanently at least. Every other week, I would go to see her. My mom and dad weren't holding hands anymore, weren't even looking at each other. They would sit across the room from each other. I guess mom was still on "vacation."

A couple years passed and I slowly lost my relationship with my mom. It was just my dad and I. I felt like I was hanging out with my best friend, but at the same time, I also felt like my best friend was a zombie. My dad would talk to me, but he was so distant at the same time. Looking back, I think my dad had a deep case of depression.

Life without Mom was hard. Our family didn't enjoy things like we did before. Christmas trees seemed to be so painful to decorate.

Thanksgiving dinners were minimal and out of a box. It was weird really, but I focused on school and playing piano for our church. Playing piano and singing seemed to be an outlet for me to let go of some of the pain that I held deep inside.

We stayed involved in the church. The church that we went to seemed to get us through this time of hardship. Our pastor at the time would invite us over to his house for lunch every Sunday. When I was 11 years old, our church lost our worship leader and the band went with him. Separation was clear in the church. The center isle seemed to be the dividing line. Bickering over carpet, who would lead worship, and how Sunday school would run were among the things that people talked about before church. Then, my Sunday School teacher asked me to start playing piano and singing for our congregation. I was extremely nervous. I was only eleven or twelve and I had no experience doing it. He said that he would work with me to help me learn the songs, so I said yes.

Every Sunday morning, Sunday night, and Wednesday night, I would lead our small congregation in worship. I think God used this to comfort me and reassure me that my life still had purpose after my parent's divorce. God was working…and life was finally starting to be normal again.

My dad didn't have much money being a non-traditional student at the local Christian college. I did enjoy, however, going to class with dad. I learned so much about Physical Science and Computer Science that I really didn't know what to do with it. I was only about 12 or 13 at the time, but I took notes just like the rest of them. I felt so "grown up" walking in to class with my dad. He even gave me a notebook so that I could take notes on what the professor was teaching that day.

I felt spoiled. My dad would pretty much buy me anything that I wanted. Not that I complained at the time, but it did effect how I acted later on in life. I got a cell phone at a very young age so that my dad could keep track of me. I liked it. I felt independent and grown up, but that spoiled life would soon come to a close, and I had little time to adjust my morale.

My dad tried to date. Oh, man, he tried. After graduating with a degree in Computer Science, he finally landed a job working for a school district. While he was there, he tried to date one of his co-workers, but it didn't really work out. It was a little awkward when we went over to her house. I would play HotWheels and Bakugon with her son, while she and my dad would talk. It was great at first, but she wasn't the one.

Then, my dad met Christina. Well, maybe I should provide some backstory here. My dad and I made an avid habit of eating at the local KFC. I really didn't understand why we had to always go to KFC. I just thought my dad liked the food, but it turns out, that's not the only thing he liked. Christina worked for KFC at the time, and she made the best KFC Famous Bowls. After trying various things, I pretty much stuck with the Famous Bowls, but only when she was working because she would put extra chicken in my bowl. Then, on one visit, I noticed that my dad started looking at her like he used to look at my mom. I was a little bit confused, but I tried to accept it. It was hard because I really didn't contact my mom much. Not that my dad didn't let me, but I got to the point where I really didn't want to. I was alienated from her.

A couple months down the road, my dad popped the question. I was surprised, but happy to see him in a non-zombie state. We had a family wedding at a small community church that we went to occasionally. Life was starting to change. I went from being the only child to being the oldest of 6 with number 7 coming a year later. It was quite the adjustment, but it was the fun kind of chaos. My dad was finally happy again, and I was beginning to see how a real family worked. Life at this point in my life was finally structured. Not that I didn't like being spoiled by my dad, but the consistency of life grew on me a little.

9 FALLING APART

The storm came quickly like wind from a hurricane. Slowly, my step mom started to verbally abuse me. She would yell at me because I wasn't doing the chores right. Not that I did it on purpose, but my parents never really taught me how to clean. It was just my dad and I for a long time and we didn't really need to clean that much. I guess she didn't know that I didn't know, you know? I dealt with it. I passed it off like she didn't understand. Secretly, I was hoping she would be willing to teach me these things because I knew I would need them later in life, and I thought it might be a way to bond with my newly found friend. At first it was a way to bond, but slowly it turned into the exact opposite. I wouldn't do something right and she would get mad instead of trying to patiently teach me the right way to do it. Most of the time it was frustrating because I had no clue how to clean, and she was Safe Serve Certified.

It went on for a long time. Our house was full of unhealthy tension. My stepmom and I would have good patches, but no matter how hard both of us tried, we just couldn't get along. We tried, oh we tried, but nothing worked. We stopped going to church, which was something I didn't agree with, and she did. The list of chores got longer and longer. The list of things I was grounded from got longer and longer, and the happy family that we started with slowly turned into a tension struck mess.

April 20, 2012, I ran away from home. My stepmom had my step-brother and I clean the kitchen after returning home from an all-day drive to pick up the other four kids. As I was sweeping the floor, my stepmom came into the kitchen. Unfortunately, I missed a spot on the floor. It was a small spot underneath the pile of dirty laundry in the laundry room off the kitchen. She saw it, and got really mad. Ok, furious. She started yelling at me, and I tried to explain that I didn't mean to miss a spot, I just didn't think to pick up the laundry and sweep underneath. She was still mad, and, after having a huge argument, she told me to take a walk outside at one o'clock in the morning. So I did.

Tears streaming down my face, I walked along the side of the highway in the middle of the night. It was April, so the air had a slight chill, but luckily I grabbed my jacket before I left. I didn't know what to do. I was literally crying out to God, asking where he was and what he was doing. I was furious at him. I found it so easy to blame him for what I was going through, when in reality, it was mostly my fault. I didn't do chores exactly like I was told. I would sometimes change it ever so slightly so I didn't have to do as much. Of course, my sneaky way of doing this was almost always caught. I felt like I was working too hard. I felt like I couldn't handle everything they were having me do.

Bright lights came around the bend as I wondered through the night. As the car passed, I hoped that it wasn't a cop or anyone that I knew because I really didn't feel like explaining the situation. Then I heard the car slow down and make a U turn. I have never been so afraid in my life. Then I heard a familiar voice cut through the midnight air. It was one of my friends from school. As he pulled his

Jeep beside me, I tried to compose myself. It didn't work. He asked what was going on, and I lost any composure that I had tried to muster. I tried to explain the situation in between sobs.

As I climbed into the car he explained that he didn't have room for me to stay at his house. I didn't expect him to. I really was clueless as to where to go. He ended up taking me to my pseudo girlfriend's house. (I had a big crush on her, and I was kind of clueless, wondering if she felt the same.) Anyway, we were good friends, nevertheless. I didn't know what to think as I awkwardly knocked on her door at 1 o'clock in the morning. "What if she doesn't answer?" What if she does…with a shotgun?" "What if her mom answers and starts yelling at me too?" After about 15 or 20 minutes of knocking and ringing the doorbell, her mom answered the door. I went on to explain the situation, why I was standing on her doorstep at such an early hour. She understood and invited me to stay in the spare bedroom. As I sat on the bed, my heart got colder and colder. I started asking God questions.

"Why would you let this happen to me?"

"What did I do to deserve this?"

"What do you want me to do NOW, God?"

I was confused and frustrated to say the least. Then, Ashley knocked on the door. We talked for an hour or two or three. I couldn't really keep track of time that well. Then, she pulled out her Bible and started reading from Psalm 18. It read:

"I love you, O LORD, my strength. 2 The LORD is my rock, my fortress and my deliverer; my God is my rock, in whom I take refuge. He is my shield and the horn of my salvation, my stronghold. 3 I call to the LORD, who is worthy of praise, and I am saved from my enemies." (NIV)

To this day, this is my favorite scripture. I have held onto this my entire life and will never forgot God's amazing grace in life's difficult situations.

I stayed the weekend there. The next day we had to take her dog to the vet. If I remember right we had to get his nails clipped, which was very painful for the dog, but, perhaps more painful for Ashley as she watched her dog whimpering in pain.

Monday morning came bright and early. As we jumped into Ashley's Mustang, I got more and more nervous. The thought of my dad showing up with the entire police department and possibly the Air Force, crossed my mind. I really didn't know what to expect.

Walking into the school was different. Normally, I was the quiet, reserved person that always sat alone at lunch. Now, I was the kid who ran away from home over the weekend. Thankfully, not everyone knew. I'm sure some people knew but it wasn't really evident. As I entered my first block class, I didn't know how to look at my classmates. It was too weird. Then, right after the bell rang:

"John Caldwell, please come to the office. John Caldwell to the office. Thank You."

It was even more embarrassing coming over the intercom. I gathered my things, and slowly walked to the office.

My dad was waiting there for me. I bit my tongue as my dad put on the act.

"I really don't know why he ran away."
"I promise I will keep him under control."

He acted as if I was a monster, or a pet dog. I bit my tongue until we were escorted into a conference room to "resolve our issues." Then, I spewed. I told my dad that I was done acting as a slave and I was done living in such a stressful situation. He brushed it off, like I was being unreasonable. In tears, I followed him out to his car. I went to work with him for the rest of the day. I didn't know what to say to him to make him see what I was feeling, so I said nothing. Apparently, he already had a plan because when we got home, we switched vehicles, and my dad started driving. My stepmom had already packed all my clothes while I was at work with my dad. Nobody told me where we were going. I slowly figured out that we were going to my grandfather's. He lived a couple hours away in the same town as my uncle.

When we arrived, I didn't know how to react. I went straight to the room, upstairs, where I would be staying. I didn't want to come down. My dad finally came up to get me so I could say my goodbyes. This had happened before. He would take me to my grandfather's to scare me and come back twenty minutes later to pick me up. This time, I wasn't coming back with him. I was so done.

I stayed the next couple months with my uncle part time and my grandparents the other part of the time. I finished my sophomore year at Yellville-Summit High School. It felt like a new environment. New people who didn't know what I was going through. New friends, a brand new start. I was even able to go to an awesome concert with the band. If I remember right, it was a Dallas Brass concert. I think I got the name right. Anyway, it was awesome!! It was the first concert that I had been to in ages. It was so much fun and I am so thankful that my grandparents let me go. I made new friends really quickly. As the school year came to a close, I found a volunteer job at the local salvage yard where my uncle worked. I have to say, I didn't think working in a salvage yard would be so enjoyable. It was awesome. I didn't really do much because I wasn't "old enough", but finally, they let me pick up tires and rims around the yard. The best part was that I could ride one of the 4 wheelers to do it!!

I finally got back into church. My grandparents and my uncle and family, were going to Summit Pentecostal Church of God. It was a church that I had visited years earlier with my dad. It was also the church where I first started to learn piano and found my voice. I guess it was God's timing because the first week I was there, they asked me if I could lead worship while their worship leader was on vacation. At first, I said no. I didn't think my heart was right to be leading even a small congregation in worship. Then, God started healing my heart. He helped me find forgiveness and compassion for my dad and step-mom. So, the next Sunday, I said I would.

I led worship for the next couple of weeks and even sang a couple of songs I wrote on guitar. It was cool, because about the time that I got there, a new fill in pastor came. The previous pastor was moving back to his home state of Idaho. The new pastor was Reverend Ted Matlock and his wife Nancy. They were the same pastors that helped my dad and I get through a tough time after my parents got divorced. When I first walked into the sanctuary and saw him, I didn't know what to say. My life had fallen apart since we last talked, and I felt like pieces of broken glass lying on the floor. After many long conversations, I explained what happened. It was hard getting it out. It's still hard. Even as I am writing this, my heart is heavy.

The summer was nearing its end, and my heart was starting to change. I kept wondering if my dad and stepmom still loved me. I didn't know for sure if they really wanted me to come back. I felt like I was missing out on so much of my brother's and sister's lives. I didn't know if they wanted me to come back, or if they expected me to stay with my grandfather until I graduated. I lost count of how many nights I cried myself to sleep. Luckily, my grandparents were at the other end of the single-wide trailer, so they didn't hear my loud sobs. At least, I don't think they did. My grandfather had a weird way of hearing things from across the trailer.

Then, I called my dad. It was mid-July, right around his payday, which was the 20th of every month. I dialed the number, and as soon as he answered, I started crying. For some reason I couldn't stop. Through my sobs, I asked him if I could come home. The whole conversation, he seemed so distant, like he was acting like he cared about me. This unsettled me. I didn't know if I was making the right choice coming back. He finally said he would come and get me when he got paid on the 20th. I said ok, and started packing up what little clothes and things I had with me.

In between the time that I made the phone call, and the time that I would be going back home, I started to pray. At first, it was hard to talk to God. I didn't know how to ask God for something after blaming him for so much. Slowly, but surely, it got easier. I prayed that he would work in my situation when I got home. I didn't know what was going to happen when I got back. I was praying that it wouldn't go back to the way it was. I prayed that God would help my parents see what I was feeling inside. Thoughts of suicide, wondering if anyone would miss me if I left.

(Sorry…I just started crying a little.)

I prayed, prayed, and prayed. I started to feel God's peace, but I had doubts. I didn't know if God was really there.

(Okay…I'm in a Waffle House restaurant…tearing up, trying not to burst into tears in front of strangers.)

So, I went back home…worried, scared, and at a loss as to what was going to happen. The ride was quiet and awkward at the same time. I didn't know what to say. I thought about breaking the silence by saying:

"So…….how's it going?"

Instead, I said nothing. The silence was unbearable. I was so worried that they were going to do something to me, or I was going to do something to me. The threat of sending me to a military boot camp was already in the air. I laughed at that. Thinking to myself that if that was the solution, they might find me gone the next morning, for good.

At first everything was great. We had a long talk when we got home. We discussed my behavior, and how it had to change. I didn't really know what to change, or how to change it. I was so disconnected from the world after being ripped out of church, the only thing that I felt kept me close to our Lord, Jesus Christ. I grew up in church. I didn't know how to cope with not going. Living life without encouragement and uplifting messages, without an example of a Pastor to look up to, without the love of Christ demonstrated by his people. I felt so empty, so disconnected from everything, even myself. I didn't know who I was anymore.

I tried to do everything they told me to, and as I did so, I felt like I was a stranger in a house full of relatives…that I wasn't related to. I remember family movie nights that would only happen when I was grounded from watching TV. Instead I would clean the kitchen while they would watch "Avengers." That was the night that the thoughts of suicide got stronger and stronger. As I scrubbed the floor with a damp cloth, I wondered if they would even miss me if I snuck out the back door.

Life dragged on as the abuse started again. Slowly, but surely, my dad and step mom would yell at me for not cleaning properly, or missing a spot on the floor. I didn't know how to make them happy. I was trying, oh I was trying. I tried to go the extra mile and clean the bathroom without being told to. Instead of thanking me, or even acknowledging my hard work, they would find any and every flaw in the work I did.

"You didn't use the right cleaner."

"This mirror still has streaks on it."

"There's a piece of hair on the floor."

I didn't know how to please them. Finally, it got really bad. One night after another long fight between my dad, stepmom, and myself, I had to sleep on an extra mattress in my father's room while my stepmom slept in my stepbrother's room that he shared with me. It was 5am, and two hours later, my stepmom tried to wake me up. I physically couldn't get up. I was too stressed and worn out by doing chores the night before, and not to mention all the fighting. She got extremely mad that I wouldn't get up. I tried to explain that I physically couldn't, and she got furious. Finally, she took the mattress that I was sleeping on, picked it up and flipped me against the desk that was at my head. I was in shock for about 30 seconds. I wasn't even half awake yet.

Then, I uttered my first…and LAST cuss word. I called my stepmom a bitch. It's not something that I am proud of at all. If I could go back and not say anything at all, I would. Then, she started slapping me. It seemed like she wouldn't stop. I finally came to my senses and got up. We started yelling at each other and I'm surprised our neighbors didn't hear us. We got loud, and finally we decided to stop. She went into one room and I went into another. Of course, my dad was already at work when everything happened.

The next couple weeks I was mad at God. I would silently yell at him every night. I didn't know where he was, or what he was doing. I told him that I prayed so much.

"Where are you NOW, God?"

"I thought YOU could fix this."

"What are you doing?"

Tears would fall off my face every night before I fell asleep

This was definitely the lowest point in my life. Thoughts of suicide passed over my mind constantly. I felt like God was done using me and now he was leaving me…

Then, a letter came in the mail. Apparently it was an important one because this was the first one that my parents read to me. I found out later that they kept all my mail. Christmas cards, Happy Birthday cards, Just Thinking of You cards. Everything, they kept from me so that I wouldn't want to contact my mom, and even when I would contact her, they would record the phone calls and question me after.

"Why is there silence there?"

"What did you mean when you said this?"

This letter was from my mom. She was asking if I wanted to

come and visit her. I was surprised because I hadn't really heard from her consistently in about 2 years or so. Then, instead of offering to let me go visit her, my dad changed the question.

"Do you want to go live with your mom?"

I didn't know what to say. I felt like that was the opposite of what my dad wanted to do because he, along with my stepmom, tried to scare me into not going to live with her. They explained the "horrors" of going to a bigger school. What they didn't know was that I was used to this. I had already attended 4 different high schools so far, and they tried to make Parkview High School in Springfield, Missouri, sound like the worst one yet.

They gave me a week to decide. I had to choose between my father and my mother. During this week, they said they wouldn't ask me, but I had to go to my dad and tell him either way before seven days were up. I didn't know what to do. I started praying again. Asking God if this was the way he was going to fix everything. I wasn't exactly sure. I went back and forth. Even wrote out a pros and cons sheet to help me decide. Then, the day before I had to make my decision, I woke up with peace about the whole situation. The abuse, the feelings of slavery, even the thoughts of suicide, all went away. It was like I woke up a new person. I can't explain it any other way than it was our Lord, washing me and my life, and providing a new beginning. Still, I had to face my dad. I had to tell him that I couldn't live with him anymore. It is still the hardest thing I have ever done in my life thus far, but I had to do it. At first, my dad was mad at me, but he understood. With everything that was going on between us, he was probably glad that I was leaving. It would relieve a lot of tension in the house.

10 RUNNING HOME

A couple of days later, I met my mom, and the people she was living with at the time halfway, which was about Harrison, AR. I packed up all the stuff that my dad would let me take and I moved out.

I now know that this was God's plan all along. As soon as I got to my new high school, Parkview High, I scouted out a practice room with a piano in it. It was in the choir room, and most days I would spend at least an hour practicing piano and singing my heart out until the choir teacher told me he was going home. It was in these times that I felt God working the most to heal my heart. Then, one day, after a shorter than usual practice, one of my friends caught me as I was coming out. "Do you think you could play a song for the upcoming assembly? We are doing an America's Got Talent theme and you would be perfect." Well, I was working on a song for the upcoming talent competition with the Nazarene Church I went to, so I said yes. I kept practicing, and practicing, and practicing. While I was with my dad and stepmom, I wasn't allowed to play piano, or even sing inside the house. If I wanted to practice, I had to go outside.

Now, I could practice however long I wanted to without interruption. I loved it, and for the next couple of weeks I put almost all my time into practicing for my performance in front of 1500 or so of my peers. I would spend hours upon hours at the school, in the practice room, practicing the song that I would perform. I put everything I had into it. Ironically, the song was entitled, "Everything", by Lifehouse. That song meant so much to me. It explained my life journey in a way that I couldn't. I had drifted away from God, but finally, by His grace, I was beginning to discover a life at a different pace. I was surrounded by people that loved and cared for me, and I couldn't have been happier with what God was doing in my life.

Talk about instant friends. My phone wouldn't stop vibrating in the class after I performed at the assembly. Facebook friend requests, text messages from the few people that had my number, and pictures of me playing were among the things that popped up on my phone. It got to the point where I had to turn off my phone so it wouldn't interrupt the class.

Life was finally starting to feel worth it. I had a "new family" so to speak. Craig and Crystal became my "adopted aunt and uncle." Miller and Andrew became my "cousins." It was just easier to explain that way. And, after a couple of months, my mom decided to move back to Arkansas, and I stayed with Craig and Crystal. My reasoning? I really didn't want to go to yet another high school. I was happy. For once in a very long time, I was, and still am happy.

My senior year came around and I decided to do everything I could to get the most out of my last year of high school. I was in three choirs: Men's Chorus, Concert Choir, and Chamber Choir, I joined the Cross Country team, mainly because I had never done a sport before and I wanted to prove to myself that I could do it, and I was also on the Speech and Debate team. Looking back on it, I had a pretty great Senior Year. I made so many friends, and, like icing on a delicious cake, I had the honor of speaking at my graduation ceremony. And, if that wasn't enough, I received just short of what I thought was a full ride to Mid America Nazarene University.

The week before I came to Mid America Nazarene University, the people I was living with, Craig and Crystal McDonald, kicked me out of their house. I was working two jobs that summer: Cashier at Mardel Christian & Education Store, and a Summer-Serve Intern at One Life Church. I had to buy my own food because apparently they didn't have enough money to buy food for me anymore. On top of that, they wanted me to basically do all the chores in the house, on top of the two jobs I was working. On Sunday, August 17th, I asked them if I could take a break and breathe a little before coming to college. They said no, but as soon as I offered them money to have a break, they were all for it.

The next day when I came home, however, they started to ask me to do things while I was trying to get packed. I tried to remind them of the agreement we had, but Crystal started yelling at me, saying that I wasn't paying rent and I should find somewhere else to live. I gathered a few things and walked out.

At first, I called Kevin, one of my good friends from church.

Apparently he relayed what was going on to my youth pastor, Robb, because shortly after I got off the phone with Pastor Kevin, I received a phone call from him. That day, I packed up everything I had, and left the place that I thought I could finally call home. I have since found a new home with my youth pastor. When we got to his parents' house, he told me that I am basically family, and invited me to come home for Thanksgiving, Christmas, and any other breaks that I may have.

Then, I went to Mid America Nazarene University to study youth and family ministry with a concentration in music. My first semester at Mid-America was great. I absolutely loved the Christian environment, the professors, and all the friends I had made. I was thriving.

However, by the second semester, things started to change. After spending the Christmas season with my new found adopted family, I came back to Mid-America, almost lost. My heart had finally found a home with the Gossens back in Springfield, and yet I was leaving all of that to continue my education at Mid-America. By the middle of the semester, I had slipped into the deepest depression I have ever endured. All of the things that I had been through hit me all at once and left me broken, directionless, and alone. There were days that I physically could not get out of bed. I would lay there and watch my life fall apart.

During this time, my roommate, Charlie, was so gracious. He didn't quite understand what was going on, but He would listen. There were times where he would invite me to go to Wal-Mart with him, go eat somewhere, or join him on one of his regular trips to QuikTrip. I was so embarrassed that I was struggling with depression. I tried everything the Web-MD website said would cure it. I went for walks, worked out a little, and did things that I enjoyed, to no avail. There were days that he would have friends over and I would just lay on my bed, having been there the entire day. I was so ashamed that I had let myself fall so far.

It didn't help that I was also starting to deal with my sexuality. At this time, I had struggled with thoughts of homosexuality for about nine years. I had never had intimate relations with another man, but I had urges and feelings that I didn't know how to deal with. I tried going to counseling on campus, but I was so ashamed and afraid of anyone finding out, that I just clammed up every single session. Finally, I told my counselor, and he didn't really have anything to say.

I left the session even more broken than when I came. The Church of the Nazarene is very much so against any thought of homosexuality. The fact that I was looking to become a minister in the Church of the Nazarene did not help anything. I felt helpless and afraid. Finally, I got up the courage to talk to my college pastor about it. We had lunch, and I finally broke it to him. We really didn't know each other that well, so I thought it might be a little safer to tell him. He basically told me that I needed counseling. At this point I thought something was seriously wrong with me. I felt as if my life was spinning out of control. I felt as if God had left me behind.

Then, the thoughts of suicide came. There were nights when I just sat in my dorm room, staring at the ceiling and crying my eyes out. I would only do this if Charlie went home for the weekend, or if he was out with friends for the night. I didn't want him to see me like I was. During this mental chaos, a lot of people reached out to me to see if I was doing okay. All of my bosses from the jobs I had on campus were concerned. They noticed something strangely different about me when I came back second semester. I couldn't even bring myself to sing, something that I had previously enjoyed greatly. My world felt like a vortex, sucking out all the life, that once vibrant, leaving me empty and directionless.

Finally, I gave in. I was going to do it. I was going to take my own life. My life had been so hard up to this point, and I felt as if I couldn't handle the weight anymore. One night, while my roommate was home with his family, I found a bottle of pain relievers in the dorm room that I had bought first semester. I was going to take all of them at once. Thankfully, I couldn't bring myself to do it. Instead, I tried wrapping my phone charging cable around my neck, cutting off most of the oxygen to my body. The next day, I reached out to my Resident Educator and told him what had happened.

We had lunch at the local Chik-Fil-A. I told him the condensed version of my life's story before we went in and sat down. It was all I could do to get it out. I told him the deepest things that I was struggling with, even the part about my sexuality. It was so hard to admit that to both myself and to him. Not that I had made the decision to be gay, but that I had struggled with thoughts and fantasies of that manner. I had this fixation on the strong male figure, and I had no clue how to handle it.

My finances weren't great either. I was working three different on-campus jobs just to make ends meet. Most of the time the jobs weren't enough to do so. It didn't help that my only form of transportation was a little 49cc scooter that only worked half of the time. First semester, I was barely able to keep my job at Mardel Christian Store in the next town over, and, by the second semester, I had released my position there.

After a lot of mental ping pong, I decided to check myself in to a mental rehabilitation facility. Oh, was that fun. The first time that I went was by ambulance. I had just woken up from a mid-day nap. I sat up in my bed in my dorm room and started shaking uncontrollably. I lost control of my arms and my hands started clenching up, my fingers mangled. Short of breath, I called 911. I told them that I couldn't breath and could barely hold on to the phone. All of the thoughts that I had the days and weeks before started rushing through my head. Thoughts of suicide, homosexuality, and my life spinning out of control were among them. I panicked. The Emergency Response Team finally got there along with Campus Security, the Resident Educator, and finally my roommate. I was yet again, embarrassed.

My first semester at Mid-America Nazarene University, I had

been, what some people would call, the "face" of MNU. I was involved in everything on campus. I had multiple jobs, I was in two choirs, in a play, and was on the ministry team for a church about an hour away from campus. Every Sunday, we would pile into a van at MNU, and head over to Drexel Church of the Nazarene. I had it all together, or so I thought. I was doing everything that I could to pay for my tuition, while still being involved. The stress of everything finally caught up with me and sent me to the mental hospital. Shortly after leaving, I decided to call Mom Gossen. I told her everything that I was experiencing and she gave me the faith and courage to keep going. I didn't really know how to explain what I was feeling, but, like any mom would, she knew.

In late March of 2015, I decided to come home. I had already missed a lot of my classes, and I was weeks behind on coursework. Looking back, running home was the best thing that I could have done. God was so faithful during all of those trials of my life. He brought me through the hardest times of my life, and now He is ushering me in to His purpose and His plan. Now, as I am writing this, I am in awe of what God has done to restore my life and my faith. I have a full time customer service job with a local bank, bought my first car, and am pursuing a local minister's license with the Church of the Nazarene. God has also taken away almost all of those homosexual urges, and has blessed me with a beautiful girlfriend. Shelby is her name, and on our first date, she explained to me her struggles with same sex attraction. Her mother is the pastor of a local Presbyterian church and her father is also an ordained minister. If God would have it, I would consider marrying Shelby and her family, but that is something that I will have to pray more about. I feel as if my life is now complete.

I am so excited to see what God had in store for my life. I trust Him with my entire being, my heart, mind, and soul. He is doing great things, and for His plans, I am eternally grateful.

11 DISCOVERING LIFE

What an amazing story that God has orchestrated in my life. As we wind down our journey together, I would like to thank you for holding on with me. Hopefully, by now you haven't put the book down and abandoned it. My hope is that you read till the end to see what God would do, and how He worked everything out for the good of a young man who loves him dearly. (Adapted from Romans 8:28).

I can't tell you how freeing and exciting it has been to write this book. Putting my story in words has been one of the most exhilarating and, at times, heart breaking experiences I have ever encountered.

Throughout my life, there have been many times that I have

wanted to give up. I have wanted to take my own life, but thankfully, by God's grace, I haven't. If you ever have these thoughts, just remember that God is always with you. If you need someone to talk to my personal number is (417)-225-0910. Feel free to call me anytime , day or night. Suicide is a growing problem both in the United States and throughout the world. If there is anything that I can do for you, let me know.

My hope is that through this book, you have been able to discover a life that has been molded by the hands of the Master. I am still, and will forever be in awe of what God has done in my own life. I pray that He reveals to you the amazing plans he has for yours. Thank you so very much for reading my book and I pray that you are able to run home to our Savior, discovering life along the way.

ABOUT THE AUTHOR

John Caldwell is a Customer Service Representative, author, pastor, musician, and follower of Christ. He likes to take long walks at parks and in the woods to experience God in nature. He is a very passionate young man that loves God and people in a way that touches lives, and restores hearts to Christ.

Running Home

John Caldwell

Running Home

John Caldwell

Running Home

Running Home

Made in the USA
Charleston, SC
23 December 2015